Hank and Diane Goor.

SKAGWAY AND DYEA, ALASKA

DO731382

GOLD RUSH GATEWAY

SKAGWAY AND DYEA, ALASKA

PICTORIAL HISTORIES PUBLISHING COMPANY
MISSOULA, MONTANA

By Stan Cohen

COPYRIGHT © 1986 STAN B. COHEN

All rights reserved. No portion of this book
may be used or reproduced without
written permission of the publisher.

LIBRARY OF CONGRESS
CATALOG CARD NO. 86-60127

ISBN 0-933126-48-4

First Printing: April 1986
Second Printing: April 1988
Third Printing: March 1992
Fourth Printing: March 1994
Fifth Printing: March 1996
Sixth Printing: April 1999
Seventh Printing: March 2003
Eighth Printing: March 2007

Typography Arrow Graphics, Missoula, Montana
Cover Design Allen Woodard, Seattle, Washington

Printed in Canada by Friesens Corporation, Altona, Manitoba

Front and back cover postcards from author's collection

PHOTO CREDITS

AHL—Alaska Historical Library, Juneau
AMHA—Alaska Museum of History & Art
D—Dedman's Photo Shop, Skagway
LC—Library of Congress, Washington, D.C.
NA—National Archives, Washington, D.C.
NPS—National Park Service, Skagway
PABC—Provincial Archives of British Columbia, Victoria
Trail of 98 Museum, Skagway
UAA—University of Alaska Archives, Fairbanks
USA—US Army Archives, Washington, D.C.
UW—University of Washington, Special Collections, Seattle
YA—Yukon Archives, Whitehorse
Modern-day photos were taken by the author

PICTORIAL HISTORIES PUBLISHING COMPANY, INC.
713 South Third Street West, Missoula, MT 59801
PHONE (406) 549-8488   FAX (406) 728-9280
EMAIL phpc@montana.com
www.pictorialhistoriespublishing.com

Contents

Goods Forwarded Without Delay.

Rates Cheap.

NELSON & ANDERSON

PACKERS AND FORWARDERS...

Skaguay to Lake Bennett.

OFFICE:
ANDERSON HARDWARE STORE.
RUNNALLS ST.

Skaguay, Alaska.

TONY STANISH

LOUIE CEOVICH

Pack Train Restaurant

OPEN DAY AND NIGHT

PRIVATE DINING ROOMS FOR LADIES

STRICTLY FIRST CLASS

TELEPHONE NO. 88

SKAGWAY, ALASKA.
CORNER BROADWAY AND SIXTH

NOTHING BUT THE BEST

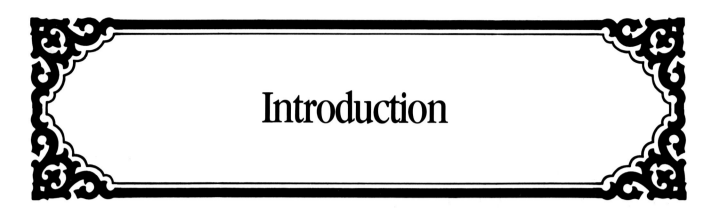

Introduction

Situated at the head of the Lynn Canal are two sites of much importance to the history of the Klondike Gold Rush, one of the greatest adventures North America has ever known. At the mouth of the Taiya River is the abandoned site of Dyea, once the major gateway to the Chilkoot trail and the water route to the interior of the Yukon. Four miles to the southeast of Dyea, at the mouth of the Skagway River, lies the other major gateway to the goldfields by way of the White Pass Trail—Skagway.

The early history of these two towns is interrelated, but today they are vastly different. Dyea has gone the way of many of the gold rush towns of the late 1800s and early 1900s—it has crumbled to the dust from which it sprang in 1897. Skagway has fared better, and along with Dawson City and a few other remains, it represents the last surviving vestiges of the gold rush. But Skagway, too, has had its ups and downs.

The fortunes of Skagway have hung on the shipment of gold and other metals from the Yukon, on World War II, on the tourist trade and the operation of the narrow-gauge White Pass and Yukon Route railroad which stretches from Skagway 110 miles north to Whitehorse. Skagway has had a fantastic, exciting, dramatic history, beginning humbly with the dreams of Capt. William Moore in 1887. Ten years later, it had exploded into a wild, frontier, gold-crazed town of 10,000, but by 1910 it had sunk to the point where only a few hundred hearty inhabitants remained. World War II, with its large military presence in Alaska, brought another boom to Skagway, and today, with a strong tourist business, its population stands at about 500.

The history of Skagway has been well-documented over the years with photographs. Most of the early day photographers who rushed to the Klondike had to pass through Skagway and Dyea; most stopped long enough to record events in the area. Names such as Hegg, La Roche, Curtis, Case and Draper, Larss and Duclos, and Barley are synonymous with the visual history of the gold rush and can be found on many photographs from Skagway and Dyea.

Other aspects of the area's history also have been well-documented with photos. The officials of the White Pass Route railroad hired their own photographer, H.C. Barley, to record the two-year construction project. Barley's collection is all the more remarkable because of the cumbersome photographic equipment of the time and the hardships encountered in building the railroad through rugged mountains.

Barley's collection is on deposit in the Yukon Archives, Whitehorse; Hegg's is at the University of Washington, Seattle; and Case and Draper's is in the Alaska State Library, Juneau. Other collections are scattered throughout the various archives of the North.

For their help, suggestions and encouragement, I wish to thank the staffs of the Yukon Archives, Alaska State Library; University of Washington Special Collections; University of Alaska Archives; and especially, Barbara Kalen of Dedman's Photo Shop in Skagway. In addition, two long-time residents and ambassadors of goodwill for Skagway, Rand Snure and Steve Hites, have been very helpful through the years as I visited the town. And finally, thanks to Richard Sims, former superintendent of Klondike Gold Rush National Historic Park, and staff members Frank Norris, Alice Cyr and Barbara Kalen for their help and review of my manuscript.

With the closing of the railroad in 1982, many thought Skagway would fade like Dyea. While this has not happened, the railroad formed a significant part of the town's history, and it has now disappeared; someday, one hopes, the railroad will return. Meanwhile, Skagway's tourist business and tour ship berthings are strong and the will of its residents is determined. The town will survive.

Skagway draws me back year after year, and each year I find something new and exciting. I hope this book will in some small way help preserve the history of this great place in the great State of Alaska.

Skagway means history!

Stan Cohen

The Photographers

Although the science of photography was in its infancy at the time of the Klondike Gold Rush, a surprising number of photographers were drawn north along with the gold seekers. Most of them stopped in Skagway on their way to the diggings, and some even set up shop in the booming gold-rush town. Despite the weight of their equipment, the remoteness of the area, and the cold and wet weather, these intrepid photographers of the gold rush managed to produce a vast collection of photos.

Probably the most prolific photographer of the era was Eric A. Hegg, owner of several photography studios in Bellingham, Wash. He headed north with the main wave of prospectors, crossed the Chilkoot Pass and floated down the Yukon to Dawson City— all the while hauling over a ton of equipment. For a time, Hegg operated a studio in Skagway, located in the present Dedman's Photo Shop.

Hegg documented every aspect of the Klondike rush from Seattle north and also participated in the 1899-1900 Nome gold rush. After 20 years in the North, he returned to Bellingham. Years later, part of his remarkable northern collection was saved from destruction by Ethel Anderson Becker and preserved for future generations.

Another of the early northern photographers was H. C. Barley, originally from Denver. In the spring of 1898, the newly formed White Pass Co. hired Barley to document the construction of the company's railroad from Skagway, over White Pass to Whitehorse. While photographing the railroad, which he did with courage and resourcefulness, Barley stayed in Skagway for two years and left the best photo record of the area. His first studio was on Fourth Avenue between Broadway and Spring; in June 1899 he moved to the corner of Broadway and Fourth.

Other photographers who became well known in the North include Asahel Curtis, Henry LaRoche, F. H. Nowell, Arthur Vogee, and the teams of Case and Draper and Winter and Pond. Together they left a remarkable record of early-day Skagway and Dyea.

Arthur Vogee's photo studio, late 1890s.
YA, Vogee Collection

E.A. Hegg, the most prolific photographer of the gold rush, had a studio on Broadway (present Dedman's Photo Shop) for a time. The dog team is ready for a 600-mile trip north to Dawson. YA, Hegg Collection

William H. Case and Horace H. Draper photographers first set up in a tent but later moved to a permanent location on Broadway. YA, MacBride Museum Collection

H.C. Barley was hired by the railroad to document its construction. His first studio was off Broadway (top) but he was soon to move into the White Navy building (bottom) on Broadway.   YA, Barley Collection

Off for the goldfields. A prospector in Skagway, October 1898.   YA

The Beginning

It was the Klondike Gold Rush of the late 1890s that put Skagway on the map, but no gold was found anywhere near the town. Rather Skagway, along with the now-defunct town of Dyea, formed an important stopping point along the route to the Klondike goldfields, hundreds of miles away.

In large part, the two towns boomed because of their proximity to two mountain passes. These passes provided a means of getting from tidewater, over the coastal mountain range, and into the Yukon's interior. A trail from Dyea led up and over the now-legendary Chilkoot Pass, while from Skagway a trail led to White Pass (sometimes called Skagway Pass).

In the 1890s, the quickest and cheapest (though not the easiest) way to get from the Lower 48 to the Klondike was to take a steamer to Skagway and then march over one of these passes to the head-waters of the Yukon River. From there, one could build a boat and float the 500 miles downstream to Dawson City and the goldfields. Skagway and Dyea, as "gateways" to the Yukon, were swarming with thousands of gold-crazed fortune hunters soon after word of the Klondike strike reached the outside world.

Skagway actually got its start about 10 years before the gold rush largely through the efforts of Capt. William "Billy" Moore. After spending years as a riverboat captain and prospector, Moore came to the North in the 1880s and took up packing, trading, and prospecting. In 1887, he contracted with William Ogilvie, a Canadian government surveyor, to pack a party over Chilkoot Pass, which had been used for years by local Indians and a few early prospectors. Moore, however, had heard about another route over the mountains and he decided to give it a try. This route led over White Pass (named by Ogilvie after Thomas White, Canadian minister of the Interior) and was a little lower in elevation and not quite as steep as the Chilkoot Trail. The journey was not an easy one, but Moore returned from it enthusiastic about the new route.

Later that year, Moore staked claim to 160 acres

William Ogilvie, Canadian government surveyor, who surveyed the Alaska/Canada border. He had the reputation of being the most honest man in the North, never seeking personal gain, and was named the commissioner of the Yukon in 1898.   UW

at what is now Skagway. He envisioned his new townsite as a possible gateway to mineral exploration in the Yukon. In fact, Moore believed that gold might someday be discovered in the Yukon, and hoped a railroad would eventually be built over White Pass.

At the townsite, Moore built a crude sawmill, a cabin, constructed a wharf into Skagway Bay, made some improvements on the White Pass (Skagway) Trail, and obtained a contract from the Canadian government for mail delivery from Juneau over the pass to the Yukon. Moore, an older man at the time, was helped in these projects by his son Ben.

Dyea, located about four miles from Skagway and the starting point for the trail over Chilkoot

Capt. William "Billy" Moore

Although he is not as well known to history as the discoverers of the Klondike gold, Moore was one of the great pioneers of the north country as well as the founder of Skagway.

After spending a good part of his life at sea, Moore came to the North in the 1880s when he was in his 60s and engaged in prospecting, packing, and trading. Aware of its potential as a gateway to the Yukon, Moore laid out a townsite at what is now Skagway and worked to improve the trail from Skagway over the White Pass. He also built a sawmill and a wharf at Skagway.

Despite all this, Moore did not reap many of the early benefits of the gold rush. When the first shipload of prospectors from the South arrived at Moore's little settlement on July 26, 1897, the miners promptly pushed him off his claim and moved his house from a town lot to a site off of present-day Broadway. Other promoters then laid out a townsite on Moore's original claim.

After the gold rush had subsided, Moore filed suit and was awarded 25 percent of the assessed value of all lots in the original townsite. He then sold his wharf to the White Pass Railroad and moved to British Columbia, where he died in 1909.

Capt. William "Billy" Moore, the founder of Skagway and an early day developer of the Yukon country. AHL

Captain Moore's original homestead cabin, built in 1887, now stands behind Kirma's Curio Shop. It was moved 50 feet west to make room for an addition to the Ben Moore frame house which was built in 1897-1899.
Author's Collection

In 1892, Moore built this house, which would later be situated in the center of the intersection of Fifth and State streets. After much argument, he acquiesced to the town fathers' demands to move it, which was undertaken on Oct. 15, 1898. It no longer stands. The present fire department now occupies the site of the Jobbing house (extreme left).   YA, Barley Collection

Pass, also was established in the 1880s. In 1885-86, John J. Healy and Edgar Wilson built the Healy and Wilson Trading Post and began trading with local Indians. This was one of only a few non-Indian structures at Dyea until 1897.

Meanwhile, prospectors had been busy throughout the North. In the latter part of the 19th century, several gold deposits had been discovered in Alaska, the Yukon, and British Columbia, but these were never rich enough to set off a major rush. It was believed, however, that somewhere in the Yukon lay a great concentration of gold.

The Klondike gold deposit was first hinted at when Robert Henderson, a long-time prospector in the North, found some color on Gold Bottom Creek near Rabbit (later Bonanza) Creek in the Klondike River drainage. He later told a man named George Carmack of his discovery and suggested Carmack try some prospecting. Carmack, a white man who had married an Indian woman and adopted Indian ways, set out up Rabbit Creek with two of her Indian relatives, Tagish Charley and Skookum Jim. Prospecting as they went, they found nothing until Aug. 16, 1896, when their pans revealed the first flashes of color of what would turn out to be one of the world's greatest concentrations of placer gold.

The three staked their claims and recorded them in the town of Fortymile down the Yukon River.

Prospector Robert Henderson.   UW

Word of the strike spread among other prospectors in the area, who quickly staked their own claims. The great stampede to the Klondike, however, had to wait for the news to reach the outside world.

William Ogilvie, the government surveyor at Fortymile, tried his best to alert government officials in Ottawa. He sent a message with Capt. Billy Moore, who happened to be in Fortymile when word of the discovery first came in, and Moore carried the message to Juneau, where it was relayed to Ottawa. The message was misinterpreted, how-

Skagway in 1895, before the discovery of gold in the Yukon. In 1887, Capt. William Moore had laid out a homestead on 160 acres of this flat, located in the Skagway River Valley at the head of the Lynn Canal. Two years after this photo was taken, the area held over 10,000 gold-crazed prospectors eager to get to the Yukon. AHL

With the Klondike strike, Skagway became a major gateway to the Yukon goldfields. In the summer of 1897, the first shiploads of prospectors from the Lower 48 began arriving at the town. Until large docks were built, the ships had to anchor offshore while small boats and lighters ferried men (and a few women) as well as goods and animals to the tidal flats. Top: AHL; Bottom: PABC

With the docks still under construction, barges were used to bring supplies close to shore. From there, wagons hauled them over the tidal flats to the new townsite.   UW

Early view of the townsite when it had more tents than buildings.   AHL

ever, and the news of a major gold strike in the Yukon went virtually unnoticed by the rest of the world.

In mid-July 1897, nearly a year after the initial strike, two ships laden with gold docked on the West Coast—one in San Francisco and one in Seattle. With their arrival came the history-making message—"Gold in the Klondike." The rush was on.

The first shipload of prospectors reached Skagway in late July 1897. Some of the men immediately set off for the Klondike, hiking the 30 or so miles up and over Chilkoot and White passes and then building boats to float down the Yukon River. They, and others behind them, would find that most of the streams had already been claimed. But other new arrivals saw that the real wealth of the North lay behind a storefront rather than in a streambed. They set up shop to supply the hordes of would-be prospectors that were pouring into Skagway, Dyea, and the Yukon.

As a major stopping point on the route to the goldfields, Skagway, in the course of a year, grew from a small settlement, to a tent city, to a sprawling, often-violent town of between 10,000 and 15,000. By the end of that first year, it sported long avenues lined with framed buildings, was served by several large wharves extending into Skagway Bay, and two companies of U.S. Infantry were stationed there. Part of the trail to White Pass, furthermore, had been improved by the construction of Brackett's Wagon Road, built by George Brackett, a former mayor of Minneapolis. Dyea, too, boomed with the arrival of stampeders eager to get on the trail over Chilkoot Pass, but Dyea could not accommodate ships as easily as Skagway and never grew as large.

From the summer of 1897, through the end of 1898, gold seekers piled into Skagway making her merchants wealthy. By 1899, however, the flood began to slacken, especially after gold was discovered at Nome, Alaska. That same year, a railroad line, first envisioned by Billy Moore, was completed from Skagway to Lake Bennett on the other side of the pass. This line, the White Pass and Yukon Route, rang the death knell for Dyea, as the Chilkoot Trail was no longer needed. The town eventually vanished.

The railroad ensured that Skagway would remain an important—though not always prosperous—gateway to the Yukon in the years to come, but Skagway's gold-rush glory days were about over by the time it was completed. By 1910, just 14 years after the Klondike discovery, the town's population had dropped to about 600, a fraction of what it had been during the heady days of '98.

THE NUGGET EXPRESS

GUIDE

—TO THE—

KLONDIKE and CAPE NOME

Gold Fields

FOR RATES AND INFORMATION
call on Agent

THE NUGGET EXPRESS

SKAGWAY, ALASKA

Broadway Street in 1897, soon after the arrival of the first stampeders. The street would soon become a center of activity for the new gold-rush town.   AHL

This unusual view shows one of Skagway's main streets in the early days. A few substantial buildings had been constructed by this time, but tents were still being used. This photo shows that Skagway was literally hacked out of the wilderness—the tree stumps in the middle of the street have not yet been uprooted.   YA, MacBride Museum Collection

A busy day on Broadway, May, 1898. In just one year, Broadway had gone from a muddy path lined with tents to a busy commercial street lined with framed buildings.   D

4, 1898

This road was the first real attempt to improve the route to the pass. It was a toll road and when the White Pass & Yukon Railway was formed, this road was included in the right-of-way. Brackett's Wagon Road was constructed part way up the White Pass Trail in the fall and winter of 1897-98.   YA

Skagway in 1900. Looking
south down State Street.
AHL

Skagway's fire department fighting a blaze in the YMCA/Presbyterian church building, 1898. Fire was the biggest threat to all of the towns in the North due to frame construction, inadequate fire equipment and long periods of cold temperatures.   YA, Barley Collection

Map of the Skagway townsite, as adopted by the city council on March 8, 1898. Surveyors were
Frank Reid and W. Thibaudeau.   D

Dyea

Until 1897, the only non-Indian structure at the site of Dyea was the Healy and Wilson Trading Post, established in 1885-86 by John J. Healy and Edgar Wilson. The post traded with local Indians until the great Klondike strike brought thousands of stampeders to the shores of Dyea, the starting point of the Chilkoot Trail which led to the Yukon's interior. Top photo taken early in the gold rush. The bottom photo was taken in 1915.

AHL, C.L. Andrews Collection

UAA, C. L. Andrews Collection

Healy & Wilson's Trading Post. Founded 1887, Dyea, Alaska.

Supplies were unloaded on the tidal flats at Dyea and then transported up the Chilkoot Trail. 1898.   UW, Hegg

Dyea Wharf, 1899.   AHL

Remains of the Dyea Wharf are still visible.

Like Skagway, Dyea sprang up almost overnight with the arrival of thousands of stampeders in 1897-98.   AHL.

By March, 1899, less than two years after the arrival of the first stampeders, Dyea's future was looking bleak. The White Pass and Yukon Route railroad was inching its way from Skagway toward Lake Bennett and would soon eliminate the need for the Chilkoot Trail. Without the Chilkoot Trail, Dyea had no reason to exist.   YA, Vogee Collection

PYRIGHT 1899   VOGEE

Dyea street scenes, 1898. Dyea was typical of the gold-rush towns that sprang up in the North—it had muddy streets and tightly spaced, hastily erected wood-frame buildings. Dyea, however, was luxurious compared to the tent cities that were the forerunners of towns like this.   Top: UW; Bottom: YA

Today a good (but twisting) gravel road leads from Skagway to Dyea, ten miles away by car. The town was located on the long, overgrown flat visible in the background. After its brief moment in history, the site has returned to its pre-1896 condition.

The greatest recorded tragedy of the gold rush occurred on April 3, 1898, when over 60 men were killed in a snowslide on the Chilkoot Trail. Some of the victims were carried back down the trail and buried at the Slide Cemetery near Dyea.

Today, Dyea is only a memory. This ruin, which may have been a saloon during the gold rush, is one of the few remaining landmarks.

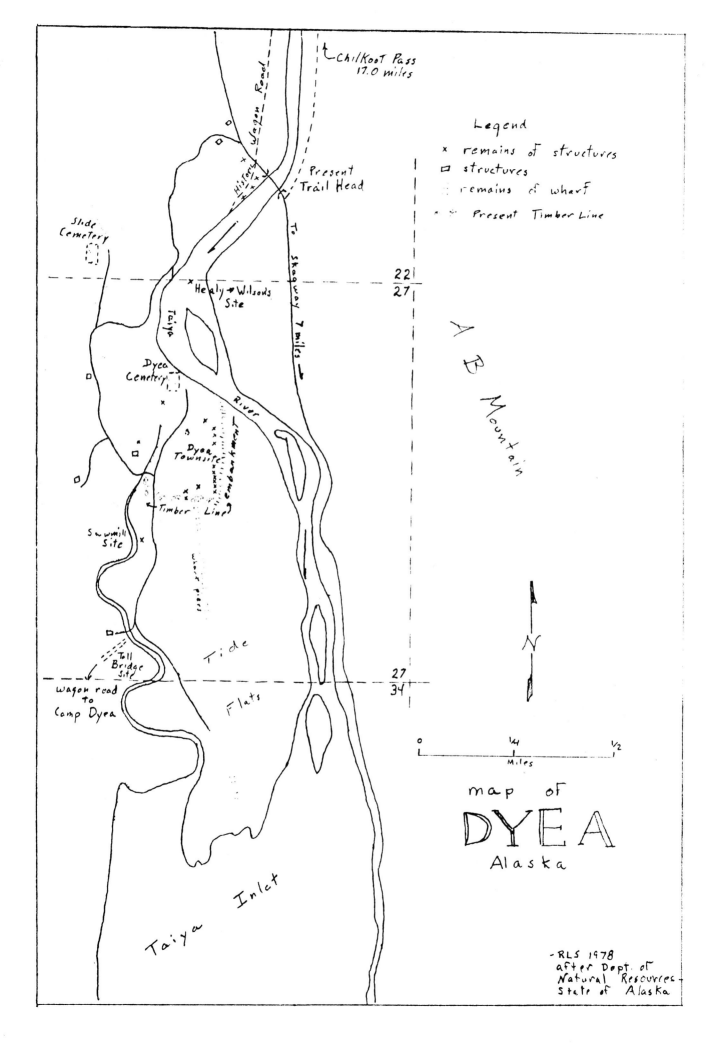

Chilkoot Pass
17.0 miles

Present
Trail Head

Legend
x remains of structures
□ structures
⬚ remains of wharf
Present Timber Line

Wagon Road

History

To Skagway 7 miles

Slide
Cemetery

22/27

Healy & Wilsons
Site

A B Mountain

Taiya

Dyea
Cemetery

River

Embankment

Dyea
Townsite

Timber Line

Sawmill
Site

N

Tide

Toll
Bridge
Site

Wagon road
to
Camp Dyea

27/34

Flats

0   ¼   ½
        Miles

map of
DYEA
Alaska

Taiya Inlet

RLS 1978
after Dept. of
Natural Resources
State of Alaska

The Passes

There was no simple way to get to the Yukon during the Klondike Gold Rush, but the routes through Skagway and Dyea and over White and Chilkoot passes were the quickest and the cheapest methods of getting there, although by no means the easiest.

The easiest way to the Klondike was the all-water route. The would-be prospector in the Lower 48 could board a steamer somewhere on the West Coast—San Francisco, Seattle, Vancouver, or Victoria—and sail north through the Aleutians to the mouth of the Yukon River, which empties into the Bering Sea. The prospector then could take a river steamer up the Yukon many hundreds of miles to Dawson and the goldfields. While this was not a difficult route north, it was very expensive and very time consuming. Few would use this.

Other routes took the stampeder overland and along various river systems through the interior of Canada. For instance, he could start in Ashcroft, British Columbia, and travel overland hundreds of miles until he reached the headwaters of the Yukon. Or he could depart from Edmonton, Alberta, follow the Athabasca River to Great Slave Lake, and then take the MacKenzie River north. These alternatives, however, were very arduous as well as

Of the 3,000 horses that were used to pack supplies over White Pass, only a handful survived. The others —victims of cruel treatment, neglect, and overloading—met their end along the trail, particularly at Dead Horse Gulch. There was great demand in Seattle for horses that could be sent north. UW

very long.

With more claims being staked in the Klondike every day, the stampeders were in a great hurry to get there. Thus, thousands of them chose to take steamers to Skagway or Dyea and then hike the trails over Chilkoot and White passes. This was the quickest way to get to the headwaters of the Yukon River at Lake Bennett. From there, they could easily float down to Dawson.

The trails were short, but they were tough. Stretching only 33 miles from Dyea to Lake Bennett, the Chilkoot Trail was very rocky and steep, climbing to an elevation of 3,739 feet at the top of Chilkoot Pass. The summit of the pass was subject to brutal weather at any time of year, and in winter it amassed snow many feet deep that could avalanche onto the prospectors at any moment. Over 60 were killed in one snowslide in April 1898.

White Pass, reached by a trail leading from Skagway, was 850 feet lower than Chilkoot Pass and not as steep, but it posed more than its share of obstacles and thus was used less than the Chilkoot Trail. The trail over White Pass was rocky and narrow, making it difficult for par-

ties to pass each other. In places, it crossed stretches of marshy ground, posing hazards to the strings of pack animals.

The trip over the passes was a logistical nightmare for the stampeders, who were required by the Canadian government to carry at least 1,500 pounds of supplies per man. Making many trips carrying small loads on his back, the average prospector took at least three months to haul his supplies from Dyea over Chilkoot Pass. Sometimes they used horses, all too often driving the animals relentlessly in their frenzy to reach the goldfields. Some of the most poignant scenes of the entire gold rush are the photos of horse carcasses piled up at Dead Horse Gulch, just below White Pass.

Despite the hardships to both man and beast, the stampeders climbed the passes by the thousands. Chilkoot Pass alone was climbed by an estimated 20,000 to 30,000 people in 1897-98. While they had chosen the "quickest" route to the goldfields, about 10,000 of them, ironically, had to spend that winter at either Lake Bennett or Lake Lindeman waiting for the ice to break up on the Yukon River.

Looking up White Pass summit from a half-mile below, March 20, 1899.   UW, Hegg

Sometimes whole families went over the passes using whatever hauling conveyance they could find.

Author's collection

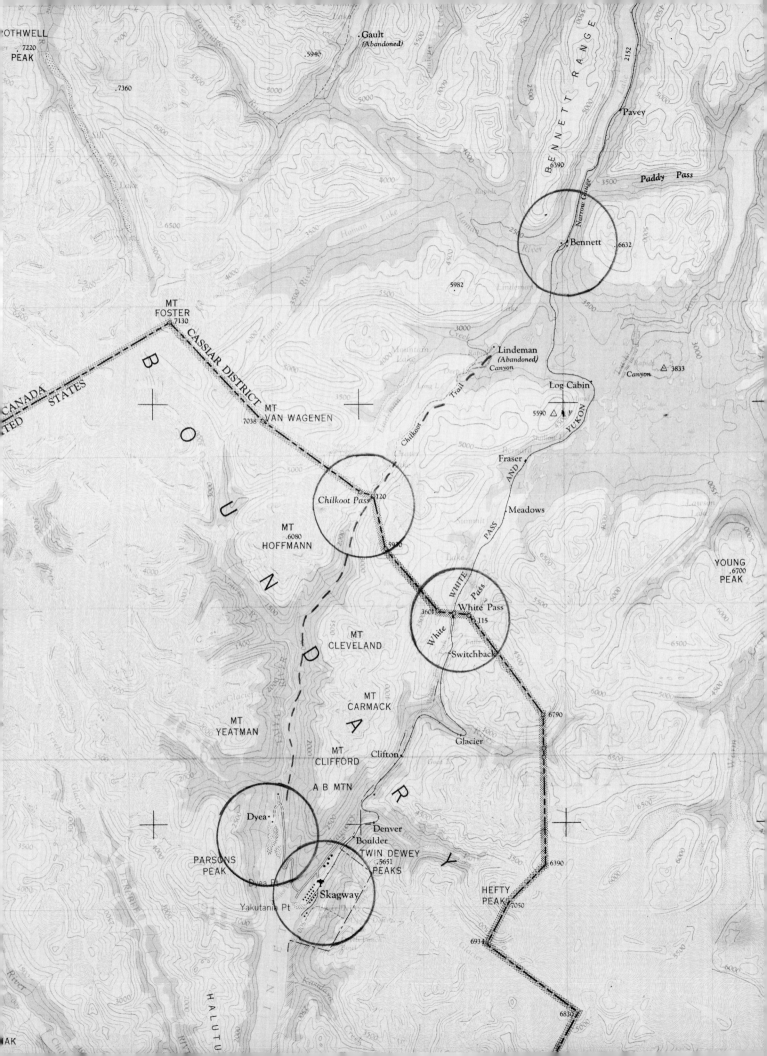

During the winter of 1897-98 the trail over White Pass became very congested with the constant stream of pack animals. The trail was narrow, with heavy forest and large boulders slowing progress.   Top and Bottom: UW

The stampeders used every conceivable method of packing supplies over the passes, including horses, oxen, and dogs. A tramway system eventually was installed on Chilkoot Pass, but travelers over White Pass were on their own.   UW

"Entertainers" heading for Chilkoot Pass on their way north.   UW

FORM P. B. 1

DYEA, ALASKA, _____189__

TO DYEA-KLONDIKE TRANSPORTATION COMPANY DR.

STEAMER		WEIGHT	RATE	BACK CHARGE	LOCAL	PREPAID	TOTAL

RECEIVED PAYMENT,

One of the most poignant scenes of the gold rush is this view showing the scales at the bottom of Chilkoot Pass, the pass, tramway and prospectors climbing the "golden stairs." The people to the right are going up and down the Peterson Route. Some people just to the right of the "golden stairs" are sliding down the snow to load up again for the climb back up the pass.   UW, Larss & Duclos Collection

President--Oscar R. Meyer, New York   Secretary--J. N. Teal, Portland, Ore.   Superintendent--F. C. Hammond, Dyea
Vice-President--W. W. Cotton, Portland, Ore   Treasurer--D. R. Strauss, Portland, Ore.   Asst. Supt. and Cashier--G. C. Teal, Dyea

Dyea=Klondike Transportation Company

Dyea, Alaska.

OF CHILKOOT PASS   COPYRIGHT 1898

Climbing up the "golden stairs" to the summit of Chilkoot Pass. Close to a ton of supplies was required of each prospector before he could enter Canada on the way to the Klondike.

Top and Bottom: UW

Street Scenes/Aerial Views

Broadway during its very early days. Compare this view, from June 1898, with later photos of the same street (pages 65 and 125). Looking north from Third Avenue.   Museum of History and Industry, Seattle.

The Kelly Block (Daily Alaskan Building) and the Occidental Hotel, shown at the height of the gold rush in 1898. These buildings were demolished in 1964. Looking south along Broadway from Sixth Avenue.   AHL

Arrival of a dog team from far-away Dawson, Christmas 1898. Note the three hotels. The St. James and Brannick were two popular establishments. The St. James is still standing, on Fourth Avenue just east of Broadway. The Golden North Hotel, seen in the background, had not yet built its distinctive dome. This was not a white Christmas for Skagway.   YA, Hegg Collection from University of Washington

Skagway in January 1898. Several long docks had been completed and the town was now established as the gateway to the Yukon.   Top: UW, WYS Collection. Bottom: Author's Collection

Deep snows on Skagway's Sixth Avenue.   Top and Bottom: YA, Barley Collection

Fifth Avenue Hotel in 1905. AHL

The Mascot Saloon on Oct. 28, 1901, during a period of high tide. AHL

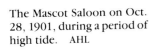

Broadway looking south from Sixth Avenue. AHL

The Dewey Hotel, which burned in 1940, is on the left; the railroad depot, now the National Park Service Visitor's Center, is on the right. AHL, Winter and Pond Collection

Looking south from near Fifth Avenue. 1913. Trail of 98 Museum

Broadway Street, Skagway's main thoroughfare, is shown in the following photographs as it appeared about the time of World War I. The White Pass tracks were laid down along the avenue in 1898 and remained in place until the end of World War II. Broadway has undergone many changes over the years, but several buildings shown in these photographs are still in existence. During its first 86 years Broadway was a dirt street; it was finally paved in 1984. Looking north from Third Avenue.
AHL Skinner Collection

Broadway Street, 1920s, looking north.   Top: D, Bottom: AHL, Skinner Collection

Top and opposite: The town was still bustling when these two photos were taken in 1900, a year after the height of the gold rush was over. The town's main business would remain the transshipment of goods and materials to and from the Yukon.
Top: AHL, Hunt Brothers Collection. Opposite: AHL, Skagway Collection

Late 1920s. Some of these buildings are still recognizable today.   AHL, Skinner Collection

Skagway's 1916 Fourth of July celebration (above) on Broadway. The building housing the Board of Trade (below) has been restored and is now the Pack Train Inn.   LC, Frank Carpenter Collection.

These two photos were taken by the U. S. Army, probably in early 1942 as barracks and Quonset huts have not yet been built. Many buildings that exist today can be seen here.   NA

Many changes can be seen in these 1960 photos. An airstrip has been constructed, the railroad no longer goes down Broadway, and several large buildings are gone. The top photo shows the old roundhouse (lower left), which burned down in 1969.   Top and Bottom: D

A 1970s view. Note the new railroad shops that were rebuilt after the fire.   D

Skagway in the 1980s is drastically different from the town of 1900. Most of the changes are found in the waterfront area, where the White Pass bulk-loading facility, the ferry dock, and a small boat harbor have been built.   NPS

Unloading lumber at Skagway, 1900.   AHL

Sylvester's Dock, 1900.   AHL

Skagway Docks

Skagway's docks and port facilities have been essential to the town's prosperity ever since the gold-rush days. The waterfront has changed considerably over the years, especially with the advent of modern dredging techniques, but it still serves as the gateway to the town. During the summer months, thousands of visitors arrive on the tourist ships that dock at Skagway nearly every day. Skagway's waterfront also provides access to the rest of southeastern Alaska via the car ferries operating on the Alaska Marine Highway. Until the shutdown of the White Pass and Yukon Route in 1982, Skagway's waterfront served an important industrial function as the terminus for ore trains unloading at the railroad's ore-storage facility.

A 1901 view of the four Skagway docks. A cruise boat is docked at Moore's Wharf.   AHL

Skagway's dock area in 1929. At one point, Skagway had four docks, but only three were left by the late 1920s, and one was falling apart.   AHL

Moore's Wharf, with graffiti prominently displayed on the rocks behind it, 1930s.   AHL

Moore's Wharf in July 1904. Note that the railroad has been extended out to and beyond the wharf. AHL, Case and Draper Collection

The caption on this photo reads, "40 vaudeville and dance house girls en route to interior of Yukon, Simons and Blake's outfit, 1905." UAA, J. B. Moore Collection

Simons and Blake's vaudeville outfit apparently took its own boat along on the journey. The boat is being loaded onto flatcars for the trip to Whitehorse. UAA, J. B. Moore Collection

Moore's Wharf about 1900. In this view, mining machinery, cattle, and hay have been unloaded and await shipment by rail to the Yukon interior.   UAA, J. B. Moore Collection

Moore's Wharf, early 1900s.   UAA, J. B. Moore Collection

A traveling ore-loader was built on the Skagway docks in the early 1900s to transfer ore from railroad cars to ships.   YA, Barley Collection

An 1898 view of the four docks that were built out over Skagway's tidal flats. Constructing these docks was a massive undertaking. PABC

Moore's Wharf after it was destroyed by fire in December 1914. It was rebuilt shortly afterward.   PABC

A U. S. Navy torpedo-boat fleet visited Skagway in 1901.   YA, Barley Collection

Three ships at the White Pass (formerly Moore's) Wharf in the 1920s. The three ships are (left to right) the CPR cruise ship *Princess Charlotte*, the cargo ship *Alameda* and the CNR cruise ship *Prince Henry*.   D

The SS *Northwestern* at Skagway. Belonging to the Alaska Steamship Co., the *Northwestern* plied Alaska's waters for many years before she was finally beached at Dutch Harbor in the Aleutians and used as a dormitory for construction workers. The ship caught fire during the June 1942 attack on Dutch Harbor by Japanese planes.   D

U. S. Navy destroyers at Skagway, July 26, 1935.   D

The German cruiser *Emden* pays Skagway a courtesy call, July 8, 1927.   D

The famous steel arch bridge spanning Dead Horse Gulch on the White Pass and Yukon Route. At one time this was the highest railroad bridge in the world.   Author's Collection

White Pass & Yukon Route

Since the earliest prospectors started coming north, railroad builders had dreamt of a line from tidewater over the mountain passes to the head of navigation on the Yukon River. As it was, prospectors, on foot, took the Chilkoot and White Pass trails from Dyea and Skagway to Lake Bennett, where boats were built for the 500-mile downstream trip to Dawson. But as the gold rush gathered momentum, the flood of people to the goldfields completely overtaxed the trail system.

The only feasible railroad route over the mountains was the White Pass. It was lower in elevation and gentler than the Chilkoot, but it still posed very formidable construction problems. These obstacles, however, did not daunt Michael J. Heney, who had arrived early on the gold rush scene with the idea of building such a railroad. Heney had already tackled some large railroad jobs, including the Canadian Pacific, and he thought he could handle this job as well.

A chance meeting at the St. James Hotel in Skagway between Heney and Sir Thomas Tancrede in the spring of 1898 led to the initial construction of the railroad. Tancrede, as it turned out, also was studying the possibility of building a railroad, having been sent north by a group of British financiers.

The White Pass and Yukon Railroad Co. was organized that same spring. The portion through Alaska was incorporated in the state of West Virginia as the Pacific and Arctic Railway and Navigation Co.; the British backers obtained charters for the right-of-way in British Columbia and the Yukon. The railroad in British Columbia was formed as the British Columbia Yukon Railway Company and in the Yukon as the British Yukon Railway Company. Samuel Graves was named president of the railroad, and construction began in May 1898. The road eventually would run from Skagway to the northern terminus at Whitehorse, Yukon, 110 miles away.

Some major construction problems lay ahead. The workers would have to deal with extreme cold and deep snows for half the construction year, and the route itself traversed mountains that were cut with sheer cliffs of solid rock and deep gorges filled

Michael J. Heney (second from left) and other railroad personnel. Trail of 98 Museum

with raging streams. In addition, construction began during the height of the Klondike Gold Rush when most of the able-bodied men were interested in mining gold and not in serving as construction workers.

The railroad builders realized from the start that a standard-gauge (4'8-1/2") railway across the mountains would be too costly, so they settled on a three-foot narrow gauge. Brackett's Wagon Road right-of-way was purchased at the start of construction.

A roadbed was built up the Skagway River Valley to White Pass City and, zigzagging up the mountains, it reached the summit of White Pass on Feb. 20, 1899. Near the summit, a spectacular steel cantilever bridge was built across Dead Horse Gulch. It arched 215 feet above the gulch and at one time was the highest railroad bridge in the world.

When the railroad reached the shores of Lake Bennett on July 6, 1899, no one would ever again have to make the arduous trip over the passes. Now a traveler could ride with his gear to Lake Bennett and take a boat to Caribou Crossing (Carcross) and Whitehorse and continue downriver to the Klondike. By the time the railroad reached the lake, however, the crest of the gold rush had passed and prospectors were turning their attention to the gold-bearing beaches of Nome, Alaska.

Still, work continued. On July 29, 1900, after 26 months of construction, the railroad finally spanned the 110 miles from Skagway to Whitehorse. The long history of railroad operation was about to begin.

White Pass trains would run regularly, weather permitting, for the next 82 years. They would haul first the gold, and later the silver, lead and zinc ore, from the Yukon to tidewater shipping at Skagway. Everyday goods and machinery were hauled north to Whitehorse, while passengers traveled both ways.

Over the next eight decades, the railroad would have its ups and downs resulting from economic conditions, wartime activity, and to some degree, political considerations. At times it would be on the brink of bankruptcy and at other times it would enjoy prosperity. During World War II it would be taken over by the United States Army.

Economic conditions, including the closing of the mines in the Yukon, finally forced a shutdown of the railroad after the 1982 season. Even the spirit of Michael J. Heney and the thousands of others who toiled on the route could not keep the road operating.

Temporary Skagway quarters in 1898 for the White Pass railway.   YA, Barley Collection

The stately railroad administration building and depot, now the home of the National Park Service's visitor center.   YA

Hotel hacks at the depot, early 1900s.   YA, Barley Collection

Clearing Broadway for placement of railroad tracks, spring 1898. The town still had a frontier character.   UW

Laying rails along the bluff in Skagway, 1898. Most of these workers probably would scatter to the next gold strike in the Yukon, British Columbia, or Alaska.   YA, Barley Collection

A view of the shops and yards during the construction phase.   YA, Barley Collection

The yards and shops in the early 1900s.   PABC

High water at the railroad shops, October 1901.   YA, Case and Draper Collection

A 1913 view of the railroad shops, located at the upper end of Skagway.   SM

UAA, C. L. Andrews Collection

WHITE PASS AND YUKON ROUTE 43

Pass one person from Skaguay to White Pass Summit and Return, February 20th, 1899, when stamped with Company stamp, to witness ceremonies connected with the completion of the tracks to Summit of White Pass.

E. C. HAWKINS,
General Supt.,
Skaguay, Alaska.

L. H. GRAY,
Gen. Traffic Mngr.,
Skaguay, Alaska.

An open-air car from the early days of the railroad. Museum of History and Industry, Seattle

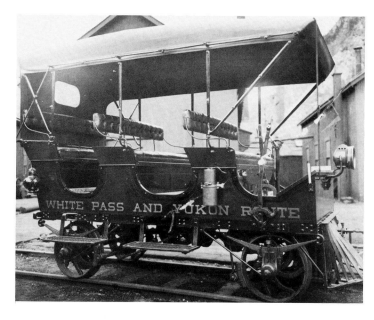

The first locomotive in Skagway, Number 2, obtained from the Columbia and Puget Sound Railway.   PABC

An early photo of railroad employees. Over 35,000 men helped construct the railroad, but only about 2,000 worked at any given time.   Trail of 98 Museum

Engine Number 7 picking up passengers at the Skagway depot, early 1900s.   UW

Broadway, 1930s. The Dewey Hotel is on the right, the White Pass office on the left. Compare this with the top photo.   AHL

Skagway train along the bluffs, early 1900s.   YA, Barley Collection

An early photo of a train loaded with 25 tons of powder, on Broadway Street.   Museum of History and Industry, Seattle

Rocky Point, high on the right-of-way of the White Pass & Yukon Route.   YA, Barley Collection

Turntable at the railroad shops, early 1900s.   YA, Barley Collection

The famous steel cantilever bridge over Dead Horse Gulch just below the summit, about 1904.   YA, Barley Collection

Engine Number 70 by the White Pass & Yukon Route station and office.   D

Diesel engine Number 93 ready for a run up the mountain to White Pass. The railroad started converting to diesel in 1954.   D

Present-day passenger terminal and gift shop.

Old locomotive sheds that were still in use when the railroad closed in 1982.

The new railroad shops that were constructed after the fire of 1969 destroyed most of the shop complex.

Businesses, Buildings, Etc.

Brouse
Bourbon

Bottled Expressly for Medicinal Use by

Mascot Saloon

A. REINERT, Proprietor

SKAGWAY
ALASKA

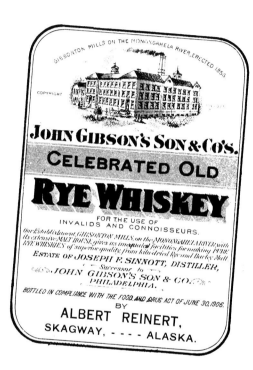

GIBSONTON MILLS ON THE MONONGAHELA RIVER, ERECTED 1855.

COPYRIGHT

JOHN GIBSON'S SON & CO'S.

CELEBRATED OLD

RYE WHISKEY

FOR THE USE OF
INVALIDS AND CONNOISSEURS.

Our Establishment, GIBSONTON MILLS, on the MONONGAHELA RIVER, with
its extensive MALT HOUSE, gives us unequaled facilities for making PURE
RYE WHISKIES of superior quality, from kiln dried Rye and Barley Malt

ESTATE OF JOSEPH F. SINNOTT, DISTILLER,

Successor to
JOHN GIBSON'S SON & CO.
PHILADELPHIA.

BOTTLED IN COMPLIANCE WITH THE FOOD AND DRUG ACT OF JUNE 30, 1906.

BY

ALBERT REINERT,
SKAGWAY, - - - - ALASKA.

LEMON SODA
MANUFACTURED BY

B. & B. BOTTLING CO.

PRICE BROS. & CO N.Y.

"The Nome"
Skagway

The Nome, located at the corner of Sixth and Broadway, was one of Skagway's most popular bars and gambling establishments. Built in 1899 and enlarged in 1900, it later became the Commerce Saloon. Today, it houses a restaurant and inn. AHL

"The Nome" - Skagway - 1898

Arctic Meat Co., early 1900s. There appears to be both domestic and wild game on display, including fish. Ernest Wolff, Missoula, Montana

ARCTIC MEAT CO.

Skagway's first drugstore, Kelly & Co.   AHL

P.E. Kern's jewelry store served as a backdrop for this picture of a collection of 250-pound mastodon tusks, excavated from the Hunker Creek area of the Klondike in 1905. P.E. Kern was one of several prominent jewelers in Skagway in the early part of the century. UAA, J.B. Moore Collection

Businesses of every description were established to cater to the thousands of prospectors heading north.   YA, Vancouver Public Library Collection

The *Daily Alaskan* was an early Alaskan newspaper founded in February 1898. It continued publication under many different owners until 1924.   YA, Barley Collection Collection

Brackett's Trading Post later became the Skagway Home Power Building.   AHL

The Trail Inn, a bar on the corner of Fourth and Broadway. The building has recently been restored.   AHL

EVERYTHING IS COMIN' MY WAY!

"Mush on" **KEELAR**

The Money King

OF ALASKA

AND LOADSTONE OF THE EARTH

Dealer in Watches, Diamonds, Jewelry and Plate

Iron Covered Warehouses for Merchandise and Baggage

BUYS PACK ANIMALS, OUTFITS AND
STOCKS OF GOODS

$5,000 Reward to the Man I Can't Trade With If He Wants to Trade

Make Your Story Short As I Am a Busy Man

BUYS GOLD
LOANS MONEY
SELLS EXCHANGE
DAILY
PACK TRAINS,
STAGE LINES
AND
DOG TEAMS

OWNS MINES.
SAW MILLS
TIMBER LANDS
TOWN SITES
STEAMBOATS and
MORE LAND
THAN ANY MAN
IN ALASKA

Frank Keeler arrived in Skagway in March 1898 and set up shop to wheel and deal in anything that would make money. He claimed to be everything from a politician to owner of gold mines, sawmills, real estate, steamboats and timber. He had "barrels of money" to loan for any legitimate purpose. He moved to this location on Broadway in 1903. The building is now the liquor store at Moe's Frontier Bar.   AAL, C.L. Andrews Collection

The Arctic Brotherhood Hall. The main structure was built in the summer of 1899 with the driftwood-and-stick facade added in 1900. Next door is the Alaska Steamship Co. building, constructed in 1900. It is now a gift shop.   AHL, Case and Draper Collection

The AB Hall later became an art shop, museum, and temporary visitor's center for the National Park Service. It is owned by the city of Skagway.   Alaska Dept. of Tourism

The U.S. Courthouse, located just off Broadway on Seventh Avenue. The stone edifice, constructed in 1899 by the Methodist Church on a portion of Capt. Moore's homesite, originally housed McCabe College, Alaska's first institution of higher education. The building itself was Alaska's first granite structure. The school closed after only two terms of operation due to the passage of public school laws, and the building was sold to the federal government for use as a district court. In the 1950s, with the discontinuance of the court, the building was sold to the city of Skagway. Today, it houses the city hall, jail, and on the second floor, the Trail of 98 museum.   AHL

The B.P.O.E. Lodge, later destroyed by fire, was located on Sixth Avenue near the Pullen House.   AHL

Kern's castle was constructed by Skagway jeweler P.E. Kern over 1,000 feet above the town in the early 1900s. With increased tourism, Kern thought his "scenic hotel" would be an ideal attraction. It is thought to be the first hotel built for tourists in Alaska. The steepness of the terrain was partly responsible for making the hotel unprofitable and the building was destroyed by a 1912 forest fire.   AHL, Case & Draper Collection

A shipment of gold from the Klondike fields, brought down to Skagway by train, is displayed in front of the White Pass depot.   YA, Barley Collection

When it opened in 1898, the Dewey ranked as one of the most fashionable hotels in town. Originally built at Seventh and State streets, it later was moved to a site across the street from the White Pass depot on the corner of Second and Broadway. The hotel burned down in 1940.   YA, Barley Collection

Bottom:
The Klondike Trading Co. built this two-story structure in 1898 on the corner of Third and State. From 1900 to 1904, the U.S. Army used it as a barracks, and in 1908 George Dedman and Edward Foreman bought the building, moved it to its present location on Broadway, added a third story and reopened it as the Golden North Hotel. Except for several years when it was closed due to financial problems, it has operated as a hotel ever since. This photo was taken about 1900 when the building stood at its original location and had only two stories.   AHL

Top:
The Golden North at its present location on Broadway. By this time a third floor had been added.   YA, Barley Collection

Numerous hotels sprang up during the gold rush to house the thousands of stampeders who passed through town on their way to the Klondike. These hotels were located in Dyea.   Top: AHL, Bottom: YA, Atlin Historical Society Collection

The Union Interdenominational Church, 1898. It was Skagway's first church and school and also served as a social club, hospital, and headquarters for the local humane society. AHL, Case and Draper Collection

Even during the early gold-rush days, Skagway was not made up entirely of businesses and hotels. Its first church opened in December 1897; the town's first churchman, a Presbyterian, was the Rev. Robert McCahon Dickey. St. Mark's Catholic Church was dedicated on Christmas Eve, 1898, and the YMCA and Salvation Army also appeared during the height of the gold rush. D

The Rev. Robert McCahon Dickey, left, and the Rev. Grant, right, with other missionaries in front of Skagway's first church, January 1898. Dickey was a Presbyterian minister who spent six months in town before heading to the Klondike in April 1898. The church, which Dickey built, also served as a school and hospital.

YA, Hegg Collection

Skagway's first school was housed in the town's first church (same building as pictured on opposite page, bottom). This is the 1898 class. AHL, Case & Draper Collection

Twelfth Avenue School, built in 1902. This view shows the 1906 class. AHL, Case & Draper Collection

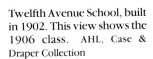

The Pius X Mission on State Street, one of Skagway's largest brick buildings, was constructed in 1933. The project was initiated by the Rev. G. Edgar Gallant, who earlier had worked for the White Pass and Yukon Route and was the first Catholic priest to be ordained in Alaska. The mission served as a boarding school for Alaskan natives from the first grade through high school. By the time it closed in 1960 the school had educated nearly 2,000 children. The building was remodeled after it was partially destroyed in a 1946 fire. It was destroyed by fire again in 1985.   D

The old Fifth Avenue theater, gone the way of many gold rush buildings. D

Herman Kirmse came north in 1897 and opened Skagway's first jewelry and watchmaking store. He was quite an entrepreneur and made several trips over the Chilkoot Pass with goods for the Klondike. His business has continued to the present day, only recently taken over by new owners, who have kept the original interior decor. Kirmse's Jewelry Store

H.D. Kirmse reportedly made the largest and smallest gold nugget chains in the world as pictured. Kirmse's Jewelry Store

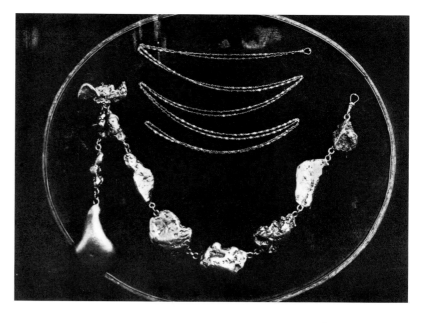

Skagway's Colorful Characters

It takes an unusual person to go charging off to the wilderness in pursuit of gold. As one might expect, the gold-rush towns—be they in the heart of the Sierra Nevadas or on the banks of the Chena River—contained their share of characters.

The Klondike rush, perhaps more so than most, included many unusual and eccentric individuals whose deeds have since been celebrated in both history and fiction. Skagway was the home of a number of them.

Martin Itjen

In the decades after the gold rush, Martin Itjen probably was Skagway's most colorful resident. Itjen came north from Florida in 1898 to join the stampede but only got as far as Atlin, British Columbia. He eventually wound up in Skagway and spent the next 40 years running a rooming house, an undertaking business, and Skagway's first Ford agency. Itjen's most famous venture, however, was the Skagway Street Car.

This marvel of transportation was built on a Ford chassis and resembled a bus. The streetcars (eventually there were four) contained a remarkable collection of gadgetry and other peculiar items, including a stuffed bear and a life-sized mannequin of Soapy Smith which would "perform" when Itjen worked a series of foot pedals. Itjen drove the car up and down Skagway's streets during the 1920s and 30s showing tourists the sights.

Never a man to let grass grow under his feet, Itjen purchased Soapy Smith's parlor in 1935 and converted it to a museum, eventually adding many Alaskan artifacts to its historical collections. The museum was later purchased by George and Edna Rapuzzi, longtime Skagway residents, who moved the building to Skagway's waterfront, where they operated the museum for several years.

Itjen was known for his sense of humor. On a trip to Hollywood in 1935, for example, he invited movie star Mae West to come north to Skagway and serve as a hostess on his street car.

Itjen died in 1942. Next to his grave is a large rock, painted gold. On it are the words, "The biggest nugget in the world."

Martin Itjen and his first streetcar.   D

The "famous" streetcar beside The Golden North Hotel.   Author's Collection

Itjen's third streetcar carried a lifelike mannequin of Soapy Smith, which could be operated electrically to turn and salute. One of the four streetcars can sometimes be viewed next to Jeff Smith's Parlor on Second Avenue. D

Sign promoting Itjen's tourist business. Taken during World War II after Itjen's death in 1942.
Mrs. Dorothy Jones
Forest Grove, Oregon

MARTIN WITH HIS STREET CAR
FOR A FIFTY CENT FARE
Will Tell You When And Show You Where
The High Spots Were. For He Was There.
He'll Start At Nine And Takes Till NOON
To Show You Skagway in The klondyke.
BOOM:
If You Miss This You Have Missed it All
And Have Not Seen Alaska At ALL
Take A Bite if You Can't Take it ALL.

BE SURE AND SEE THE MUSEUM
IN SOAPY SMITH'S OLD STATION
THERE ARE WOLF, MOOSE & MALAMUTE,
SOME HORN OF RARE CREATION.
THERE IS DAN McGREW & LADY LOU
SITTING IN THE HALL;
AND PAPERS OF REAL GOOD OLD NEWS
ARE PASTED ON THE WALL.
THERE ARE RUSSIAN BOMBS   CANOES
AND SOAPY SHOOTS OLD DAN McGREW.
YOU'LL SEE THIS FREE WITH A STREET CAR RIDE
AND IT'S THE BEST DRIVE YOU HAVE EVER TRIED

Harriet Pullen

As Skagway was at one time Alaska's largest city, it is only natural that Skagway was the site of Alaska's largest and most elaborate hotel—the Pullen House. Established by Mrs. Harriet Pullen a few years after the gold rush, it remained one of the North's leading hotels through the first half of this century.

Like thousands of other prospectors, Mrs. Pullen was lured north by the economic opportunities of the gold rush. She arrived in Skagway on Sept. 8, 1897, leaving behind a bankrupt farm and four children in Washington state. Her husband came north with her but the marriage eventually ended in divorce.

Mrs. Pullen first established a tent restaurant to feed Skagway's hungry stampeders, eventually moving the operation to a log building. Her apple pies soon made her quite a reputation, and she managed to save enough money to send for her three sons in Washington to help with the business.

In late 1897, she joined the rush to the newly found gold deposits at Atlin, British Columbia, but soon returned to her business in Skagway. Eventually, she saw an opportunity to provide the stampeders with transportation as well as food.

An experienced horsewoman, Mrs. Pullen still had seven horses down in Washington and knew she could put the animals to use packing prospectors and their supplies over the White Pass Trail. She sent for the horses, and when they arrived in Skagway she had to guide them to shore using a rowboat, as no one else would bring them in. She became one of the few women packers on the trail, and a particularly skillful one. The business, which she eventually sold, netted her a good stake for future enterprises. Her husband actually did most of the packing.

Her next project was a boarding house, and she rented a large frame house from Capt. Billy Moore. She later purchased the house and named it the Pullen House. Its tables were stocked with vegetables grown on land Mrs. Pullen owned near the old townsite of Dyea and with milk from her own cows.

Even in the years when the fortunes of Skagway were at a low ebb, the Pullen House was an outstanding hotel. For example, President Warren G. Harding visited the hotel on his 1923 trip to Alaska.

Mrs. Pullen became a well-known character throughout Alaska as well as in Skagway. She promoted tourism in Skagway, and amassed a vast collection of Alaskan artifacts. In her later years, she would relate to tourists the story of the shooting of Soapy Smith, an event she supposedly witnessed.

Two of her three sons, Dan and Royal, were decorated for valor during World War I, while her third son, Chester, drowned at Ketchikan when he was in his early 20s. After spending 50 years in her adopted town, Mrs. Pullen, a grand lady of the North, died in Skagway in 1947 at the age of 87.

The Pullen House finally succumbed to economic difficulties in the 1950s. Today, off of Broadway Street, one can still see its forlorn remains, the shell of what was once a glorious hotel.

Mrs. Pullen was an avid collector of historic Alaskana and was famous for her storytelling attributes. After her death, her granddaughter, Mary Pullen Kopanski of Seattle, Wash., exhibited the collection in Seattle from the late 1950s until it was sold by auction in 1973.

Over the years, Skagway has had many other hotels. These include the St. James, the Dewey, the Fifth Avenue, the Seattle, and the Golden North. This last hotel, still in existence, stands as a dominant building on Broadway. It was constructed early in the century as the two-story Sylvester Building, originally located at Third and State. It was moved to its present location by George and Clara Dedman and George Foreman, and a third floor was added soon afterward. It is still operated as a hotel.

Mrs. Harriet Smith Pullen wearing her ermine coat and Indian garb, early 1900s. She had arrived in Skagway in 1897, and died there in 1947.   AHL

Page 9.

Rooms Single or en Suite
With or Without Bath

Hot and Cold Water
Electric Lights
Telephone

The Pullen House
ONE BLOCK FROM POST OFFICE

Alaska's Most Famous Tourist Hotel
FAMOUS FOR ITS HOME COOKING
Milk, Butter, Cottage Cheese from our own Dairy

Rooms, $1.50 and up
Meals, $1.00

MRS. H. S. PULLEN, Prop.
SKAGWAY, ALASKA

Two views of Mrs. Pullen and her famous hotel, the Pullen House. The hotel had once been the residence of Captain Moore and his family. Through the years it was remodeled extensively, as can be seen in the changes in the porch in these two photos. In the 1920s the Fifth Avenue Hotel was moved and connected to the hotel's north end. An enclosed porch was also added.
Top: D; Bottom: YA

Captain Moore sitting on the porch of his former home, July 26, 1904. This house, built in 1899-1900, became the property of Mrs. Pullen, who converted it to the famous Pullen House soon afterwards. She added on to the house through the years and moved two buildings to her property for annexes.   UAA, J.B. Moore Collectin

Capt. Moore built this two-story bay-windowed office building in 1898 on State Street. He used the second floor himself while renting out the first floor. In July 1903 he moved the building to his lot next to his house (later the Pullen House). It was later a private residence, an annex to the hotel and after remodeling in 1936, two apartments. It is now vacant. UAA, J. B. Moore Collection

These were the remains of the once-elegant Pullen House, which stood just off Broadway. Over the years vandalism and fire took their toll on what was once Alaska's finest hotel and now nothing is left. The hotel remained open until 1957, ten years after the death of Mrs. Pullen. NPS

Mollie Walsh

Skagway has had its share of legendary characters, but few of them have been women. On Sixth Avenue, just off Broadway stands a monument to one such lady—Mollie Walsh.

She arrived in Skagway from the brawling mining town of Butte, Mont., in October 1897. After spending the winter of 1897-98 in Skagway, she set up a grub tent that spring at Log Cabin along the White Pass Trail. There she served meals to miners passing along the trail.

Many admirers came to her tent door, one by the name of Jack Newman, an important packer on the trail. For a time, she and Newman saw a lot of each other, but she broke up with him after Newman shot a Skagway faro dealer in an argument over Mollie's affections. Mollie eventually married another well-to-do packer named Mike Bartlett, and the two of them moved to Dawson and later to Seattle.

In 1902, Bartlett murdered Mollie because of her affections for another man. Newman, who had never forgotten her, erected the monument in 1930 as a memorial to his former love.

Mollie Wash's story is there for all to see to this day.

Molly Walsh.   Alaska Travel Division

Soapy Smith

Jefferson Randolph "Soapy" Smith probably ranks as Skagway's best-known character from the gold-rush days. Certainly, he was its most notorious con man. It is said that at the height of the gold rush, Smith and his gang virtually controlled the town, a reign that ended in a shoot-out with one of Skagway's leading citizens, Frank Reid.

Smith was born in Georgia in 1860 to parents who were both members of prominent Southern families. Smith spent most of his formative years in Texas, where his family moved in the 1870s. After his father, a lawyer, fell on hard times, young Jeff was forced to earn a living as a delivery boy and as a runner for a hotel, a job in which he rustled up customers and thus discovered his natural gift for speech.

When still in his teens, Smith hired on as a trail hand on cattle drives, and spent several years drifting about the West. He eventually learned sleight-of-hand tricks and made a living in the mining camps with gambling games such as the pea-under-the-shell game. He acquired his nickname "Soapy" from a game which involved hiding large bills in bars of soap.

Jefferson Randolph "Soapy" Smith.   Denver Public Library Western History Dept.

Guarding Prisoners

Reids Funeral Cemetary

The Victim

Soapy Smith at Morgue

Actors and Scenes in the Soapy Sm

Soapy Smith July 4th 98

A montage of photos depicting Smith's gang and his shootout with Frank Reid.   Author's Collection

Soapy Smith, Skagway, Alaska July 4, 1898

Soapy Smith, July 4, 1898.   D

Slim Jim

Boners
Jackson
and
Tripp

tal

gedy

Autopsy on Smiths body

Above: Jeff Smith's Parlor decked out for the July 4, 1898, celebration. Some of his henchmen are lounging in front. The building, originally on Sixth Avenue, was bought by George Rapuzzi and moved to its present location on Second Avenue in 1964.   UAA, Mackay Collection

Below: Frank Reid.   Author's Collection

Smith, who was generally opposed to violent methods, graduated to larger operations, and set up in Denver where he formed a gang. In Denver, he acquired a wide reputation for his con games as well as for his generosity to charities, churches, and those in desperate need. Also in Denver, he married a singer by the name of Anna Nielsen, whom he kept insulated from his "public" life and who eventually bore his children.

About 1890, Smith set up operations, including a gambling hall, in Creede, Colo., a wide-open mining town, but eventually returned to Denver. After numerous run-ins with the law and local politicians, Soapy Smith quit Colorado and, in October 1897, arrived with his gang in Skagway, apparently with intentions of "taking over" the town.

Working out of an establishment called Jeff Smith's Parlor, an oyster parlor that also offered liquor and gambling, Smith and his gang soon were operating their con games, as well as taking part in some outright robbery, running a protection racket, and overseeing businesses like Smith's "Telegraph Office." This last business, which charged $5 to send a message anywhere in the world, might have been legitimate but for the fact that Skagway had no telegraph lines.

Despite his lawless ways, Smith was liked and respected by many for his charity, which included organizing a program to adopt stray dogs. The townspeople, however, had no use whatsoever for his gang. Eventually, several of Skagway's leading citizens formed a vigilante-style "Committee of 101" to rid the town of its criminal element. Among the committee's founders was 54-year-old Frank Reid, a former Indian fighter and surveyor who helped lay out the original town.

The showdown between Soapy Smith and Frank Reid began when a young miner, J.D. Stewart, arrived in Skagway from the Klondike carrying $2,700 in gold. Somehow, and apparently with the help of someone, Stewart and his gold parted ways. The Committee of 101, hearing Stewart's loud complaints, suspected Soapy Smith and his gang and on July 8, 1898, called a meeting on the Skagway wharf to take action.

Soapy Smith tried to force his way into the meeting, but found his path along the wharf blocked by Frank Reid. After a brief struggle the two exchanged gunfire and both fell to the deck. Smith died immediately of a bullet through the heart; Reid lingered 12 days longer.

With the death of Soapy Smith, the law-abiding citizens of Skagway got rid of other members of the gang. Most of them were shipped south, and many served time in prison. Smith and Reid were buried near each other in the Skagway cemetery, with Reid's tombstone bearing the words, "He gave his life for the Honor of Skagway." Soapy Smith's tombstone became a favorite among souvenir seekers, who believed a piece of the stone would bring them good luck.

Soapy and some of his henchmen in his parlor on July 4, 1898. From left; Nate Pollock, the bartender, John Bowers, John Clancy, Smith, the Sweeney Kid, and someone known only as "Red." Notice the Cuban and American flags over the bar. This was during the Spanish-American War period. D

J. D. Stewart.   Author's Collection

More of Soapy's men pose for a photographer.   Author's Collection

FREEDOM

FOR

CUBA.

REMEMBER
The Maine!

Compliments of . . .

THE SKAGUAY
MILITARY CO

JEFF R. SMITH, CAPT

Smith formed a military company in 1898 and offered to take it to Cuba during the Spanish-American War. He was killed before any action was taken, if indeed his intention was really to fight for his country.
Courtesy City of Skagway Museum

One of many gravestones of Soapy Smith. Souvenir hunters have chipped away several of these through the years.   D

Present-day views of the graves of Frank Reid and Soapy Smith at the Skagway Cemetery. Author's Collection

Life in Skagway

The White Pass and Yukon Route sponsored several sports teams over the years. Pictured is its 1901-02 basketball team.   YA, Barley Collection

Capt. William Moore stands in front of his original house, built in 1892 and decorated here for a Fourth of July celebration. He lived in a log cabin previous to 1892.   YA, Vancouver Public Library Collection

Knights of the Moccabees fraternal organization celebrating July 4, 1899, in Skagway.   YA, Barley Collection

The interior of an early Skagway home, 1909.   AHL

Arctic Brotherhood dinner, 1905. The Arctic Brotherhood was a civic group formed of Skagway's pioneers.
                                                                                                    AHL

America's favorite pastime was popular even in the North. A Skagway baseball game in the early 1900s. Note the large crowds lining the field.   YA, Barley Collection

UNMARRIED FOLKS FAREWELL DANCE TENDERED TO F.F.W. LOWELL
MARCH 7 1908   DRAPER & CO.

The caption on this photo states that it is an unmarried folks farewell dance tendered to F.W. Lowell, March 7, 1908. Held in the A.B. Hall on Broadway Street.   AHL

The Military Presence

The military played a prominent role during two phases of Skagway's history—during the Klondike Gold Rush, when the U.S. infantry was called in to maintain law and order in both Skagway and neighboring Dyea; and during World War II, when the town became a major shipping center for military construction projects that were underway in the Yukon and Alaska interior.

Some of the most important troops stationed in the Skagway area during the gold rush were the detachments of North West Mounted Police which manned the summits of White and Chilkoot passes. Here, at the border between the U.S. and Canada, the troops established customs posts, ensuring that each stampeder to the goldfields possessed the requisite 1,500 pounds (popularly called a "ton of goods") of supplies—enough to last a year.

The first U.S. troops arrived in Skagway on March 1, 1898, near the height of the gold rush. Four companies of the 14th Infantry from Washington state's Vancouver Barracks had been sent north, and two were stationed at Dyea and two at Skagway. They handled tasks such as settling labor disputes and maintaining order along the Brackett Wagon Road.

Soon after they arrived in Skagway, however, some of the troops were ordered to the Spanish-American War, which was being fought at the time

U.S. troops, of the 14th Infantry out of Vancouver Barracks, Wash., set up camp at Skagway in 1898.   Trail of 98 Museum

of the Klondike Gold Rush. As they boarded their ship for the journey south, the troops received a wild send-off party that had been organized by the notorious con man Soapy Smith, who was also known for his patriotism. (Smith earlier had put together his own volunteer company, and offered it for duty in the war; the War Department refused his generosity.)

Some of the troops remained stationed at Dyea, and in the spring of 1899, these were relieved by Company L of the 24th Infantry, which at the time was one of the Army's four black units. There was less need for these troops because the gold rush had begun to wane, but they did help maintain order in labor disputes during the construction of the White Pass Route.

The black unit, which moved its headquarters from Dyea to Skagway, was relieved in 1902 by the Coast Artillery's 106th Company from Fort Lawton, Seattle. The 106th was replaced by the 8th Infantry, then by the 3rd Infantry, which eventually was taken out of Skagway, and military activity ceased until World War II.

During the war, Skagway became an important military site, and the town, which had suffered considerably during the Depression, underwent a second boom reminiscent of the days of '98. As in the gold rush, Skagway's importance was again due to its location as "gateway" to the Yukon interior. This time, however, it was not the narrow mountain trails that provided the transportation link, but the White Pass Route railroad.

The railroad was needed to haul supplies for construction of the Alaska (Alcan) Highway. Prompted by the threat of a Japanese invasion of Alaska, the 1,500-mile highway would provide a road link between Alaska and the outside world. The proposed route was accessible at only three points: at the highway's southern terminus at Dawson Creek, British Columbia; at the northern terminus at Fairbanks; and at Whitehorse, which was accessible by rail from Skagway. Men and materials for construction of the Alcan Highway could be shipped to Skagway by boat, hauled to Whitehorse on the railroad, and then moved north and south along the proposed highway route. The railroad also was needed to haul supplies for the CANOL project, the construction of an oil pipeline by the U.S. Army from Norman Wells, Northwest Territories, to a Whitehorse refinery used by the military.

Immediately after highway construction began in March 1942, it became clear that more help would be needed in running the railroad, which, with outdated equipment and a roadbed that was in poor repair, simply couldn't handle the flood of men and material destined for Whitehorse. Thus the U.S. government leased the railroad, and the U.S. Army, with its 770th Railway Operating Battalion, took over its operation. The railroad's civilian employees were retained and worked alongside the military.

With thousands of troops and tons of materials coming through town during the war, Skagway became the bustling place it had been during the gold-rush days. The Army constructed numerous buildings to house troops as well as store materials that were awaiting shipment to Whitehorse. At the height of operations in 1943, dozens of trains made the trip from Skagway to Whitehorse each day. In 1943 alone, the White Pass Route carried over 280,000 tons of material, and by the end of the war, the railroad had accumulated 36 locomotives and nearly 300 freight cars.

With the end of the war, the hectic pace of construction and shipping slackened. On May 1, 1946, the 770th Railway Operating Battalion turned over the reins of the railroad to its pre-war management. The military left Skagway soon after the war, and hasn't returned since.

Close order drill for infantry.   AHL, Hunt Bros. Collection

Troops of the 14th Infantry marching down Main Street in Dyea, 1898. UAA

Members of the 24th Infantry prepare a Christmas dinner in Skagway. The troops found little to do in Skagway, especially after 1900 when the gold rush was essentially over. They were finally relieved in 1902 by a Coast Artillery unit from Seattle which stayed in Skagway until 1903. YA, Barley Collection

Like its railroad, Skagway's main dock (formerly Moore's Wharf) was heavily over-worked during the war years. Supplies and personnel for both the Alcan Highway and the Canol pipeline project were funneled through Skagway on their way to Whitehorse.   USA

Two machinists of the 770th Railway Operating Battalions. They are Cpl. Albin Sandstrom of Superior, Wisconsin, formerly with the Great Northern Railroad, and Cpl. Michael G. Miatovick of Tracy, Colorado, formerly with the Southern Pacific. USA

An aerial view of the main part of Skagway in 1943 at the height of the highway and pipeline construction period. Every available space was used for housing and storage buildings.   D

By April, 1945, when this photo was taken, the tide of war had already passed beyond Skagway and Alaska.   USA

Train leaving Skagway for Whitehorse, December 1942. USA

Pulling into town after a run to Whitehorse, December 1942. USA

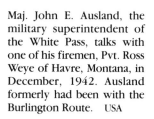

Maj. John E. Ausland, the military superintendent of the White Pass, talks with one of his firemen, Pvt. Ross Weye of Havre, Montana, in December, 1942. Ausland formerly had been with the Burlington Route. USA

Sgt. William Howard, conductor on the railroad, collects a ticket from Miss Margaret Johnston at Skagway, December 1942.   USA

Sgt. Xaviour A. Athey, an MP, checks credentials of passengers on board a train heading for Whitehorse, December 1942.   USA

Loading supplies in Skagway for shipment to Whitehorse and to the Alcan Highway construction project, 1942. LC

Terrific snowstorms sometimes hampered the railroad in winter. With the tremendous amount of freight hauled by the railroad between 1942 and 1945, it was sometimes impossible to keep the tracks open. Snow and ice would pile up many feet deep.   USA

Even large snowplows could have trouble cutting through the deep drifts. When wet snow fell and the temperature dropped, the snow froze as hard as concrete. In this view from 1944, soldiers try to repair a damaged snowplow.   USA

Aerial view of the Skagway dock and facilities, May 1945. A large portion of the materials for the Alcan High-way and Canol pipeline projects came through this dock on their way to the Yukon interior.   USA

Troops of Company B, 770th Railway Operating Battalion, at the Skagway roundhouse, March, 1944.   D

In 1942-43 the railroad ran day and night to supply the interior of the Yukon with construction material.   USA

The White House, an old hotel, was taken over by the Army and converted to a hospital in 1942.   USA

Army tents located on the old airstrip.   Trail of 98 Museum

One of Skagway's early residents, Robert (Bobby) Sheldon constructed Alaska's first automobile at the Northwest Light and Power Co. in Skagway after seeing photos of them. He used whatever materials he could find and first drove it in the July 4, 1905, parade. The top photo shows Sheldon at the controls. The bottom photo has Fire Chief and Secretary Sheldon decked out for a parade.   AHL

A Potpourri of Views

Sheldon's original car is now on display at the University of Alaska Museum in Fairbanks. Sheldon moved on to Fairbanks, operated a stageline to Valdez, was an early concessionaire at Mount McKinley National Park, postmaster at Fairbanks and state legislator.

White Pass employees sitting around a homemade vehicle constructed from train parts. It is anyone's guess what the sign means.   YA, Alaska Historical Collection

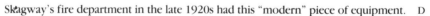

Skagway's fire department in the late 1920s had this "modern" piece of equipment.   D

The first aviator to land in Skagway, July 6, 1922. Mrs. Pullen (left), with the white hat, was there to greet him.
Trail of 98 Museum

An early biplane lands at the Skagway "Airport," which was usually the baseball diamond. Note the white flags placed in the field to mark off the runway. Skagway now has daily air service to Juneau and points south.   YA Dennet/Telfer Collection

In September 1902 a man attempted to rob the Canadian Bank of Commerce in Skagway. He brought in a bag of dynamite and told the teller he would set it off if he didn't get money. The robber got excited when someone came into the bank and he accidentally set off the dynamite, killing himself. A great amount of damage was done.   AHL, Case & Draper Collection

Skagway's last reminder of Soapy Smith was painted on the rock above the White Pass dock in 1926.

Author's Collection

A group of grade school children inspect the carcass of a whale washed up on the Skagway beach and enclosed by a board fence.   YA

FRYE-BRUHN CO.

Packers and Jobbers of

Fresh Meats

Poultry and Provisions

Fish and Game In Season

Special Attention Given to Mail Orders

P. O. Box 246

SKAGWAY,   ALASKA

Skagway
Alaska

THE ONLY GATEWAY TO THE INTERIOR OF ALASKA AND THE YUKON

THE IDEAL PLACE TO BUILD A HOME PLENTY OF ROOM FOR ALL

Compiled by
PHIL ABRAHAMS
Established 1897
For Information Write

Skagway An Outfitting Center

Skagway is the supply point for the miner, prospector and the homeseeker. The merchants carry large stocks of goods in every line, and it has been demonstrated to those who have outfitted in the States, that after paying freight and other charges to have their outfits landed at the Skagway wharf from the ship, that they could have saved in good hard cash not less than twenty-five per cent. Anything that can be purchased in the lower coast cities can be bought here, and for less money. You can buy groceries, hardware, clothing, boots, shoes, fur robes, drugs. and everything that is necessary for an interior trip, to much better advantage, and the merchant here can tell you what you ought to have, and what you ought not to have, much better than those who have not had the Alaska business experience in outfitting.

The White Pass Railway

Will take you over to any point so that you may make connections for the Atlin gold mining camp, Whitehorse, Dawson, and any point on the Yukon river. And by coming to Skagway you will find that this is the only real gateway to the interior of Alaska.

Mining

To the prospector, there is ample opportuniry for him at and near Skagway; there are good openings, and somewhere nearby the lucky man will strike it rich. So far the mountains have hardly been scratched, and that the mineral is there, there is no doubt.

GENERAL OFFICES   WHITE PASS and YUKON ROUTE   BROADWAY DEPOT

MASCOT SALOON   PACIFIC CLIPPER LINE OFFICE   BOAS TAILOR & FURRIER SHOP   FREDERICK VERBAUWHEDE CONFECTIONARY

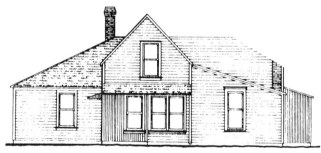

J BERNARD MOORE HOME

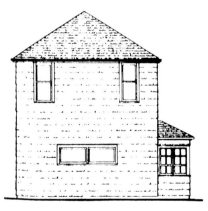

PENIEL MISSION

CAPTAIN WILLIAM MOORE CABIN

GOLDBERG CIGAR STORE & CONFECTIONARY

Drawings courtesy of National Park Service

Modern Day Skagway

In some ways, the gold rush never really ended for Skagway—through tourism, the town today reaps major economic benefits from its gold-rush heritage.

Skagway's tourist industry started way back in the 1890s with the arrival of the occasional cruise ship, but tourism did not become a big business until decades later. In the intervening years, Skagway was a major shipping terminus for goods being transported to and from the Yukon interior.

After the gold rush ended about 1900 and Skagway's population shrank from some 10,000 to about 600, the town was kept alive by the White Pass and Yukon Route. In summer, the Yukon interior was accessible via the Yukon River, but in winter Skagway and the railroad provided the Yukon's only transportation link to the outside world. The railroad hauled thousands of tons of minerals, including gold, from the Yukon's mines to ships waiting at the Skagway docks.

The Depression hit Skagway hard, but the war years brought another boom with the construction of the Alcan Highway and the Canol pipeline. After the war, Skagway entered a period of relative economic stability and continued to serve as a terminus for mineral shipments—mainly lead and zinc—from the Yukon.

Meanwhile, tourism, which had been promoted by oldtimers such as Mrs. Pullen and Martin Itjen, continued to grow. As early as the 1930s, Skagway had been proposed for inclusion in a national park, but it was not until 1962 that the town was listed on the National Register of Historic Places. Finally, in 1976 President Gerald Ford authorized the establishment of the Klondike Gold Rush National Historic Park, which was dedicated on June 4, 1977. By this time, much of the "old" Skagway had disappeared, but a number of original structures from the gold-rush days were still standing. Some of these had been moved during the 1900-1915 period to a concentrated area along Broadway Street.

In recent years, Skagway has become less of a shipping terminus and more of a tourist town. Due to economic conditions, mining activity in the Yukon dropped off over the years, and the White Pass railroad no longer was needed to haul the Yukon's minerals. Likewise, a new road from Carcross, Yukon, to Skagway cut into the railroad's passenger business. In 1982, the White Pass and Yukon Route, Skagway's economic mainstay for many decades, made its last run.

Is today's Skagway a ghost town? Far from it. Certainly it is not the wide-open boomtown of the gold-rush days or the busy shipping center of World War II. But, far from being "ghosty," Skagway is a lively tourist town. Each summer, its gold-rush attractions draw thousands of visitors who arrive via tour boats and ferries, or by automobile on the highway from Canada. In the winter, of course, life slows down for Skagway's 500 permanent residents, just as it does for other inhabitants of this part of the world.

No, Skagway is not "ghosty." Rather, it is a living piece of history that portrays the great Klondike Gold Rush of 1897-99.

Martin Itjen's grave at the Skagway cemetery. His legacy of humor is evident in his gold-painted rock behind his tombstone.

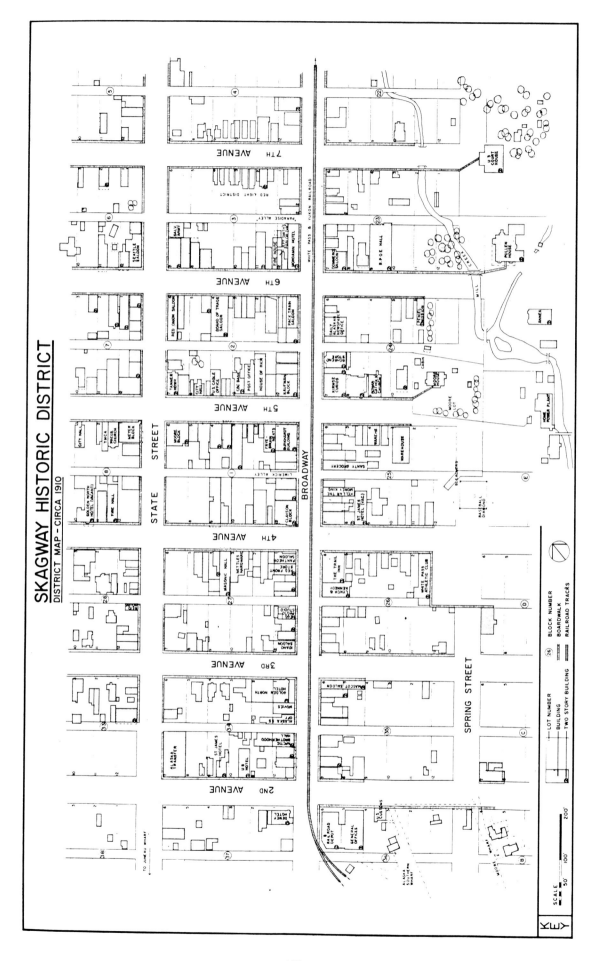

Maps courtesy of National Park Service   Many of Skagway's gold rush era buildings (shaded) still exist.

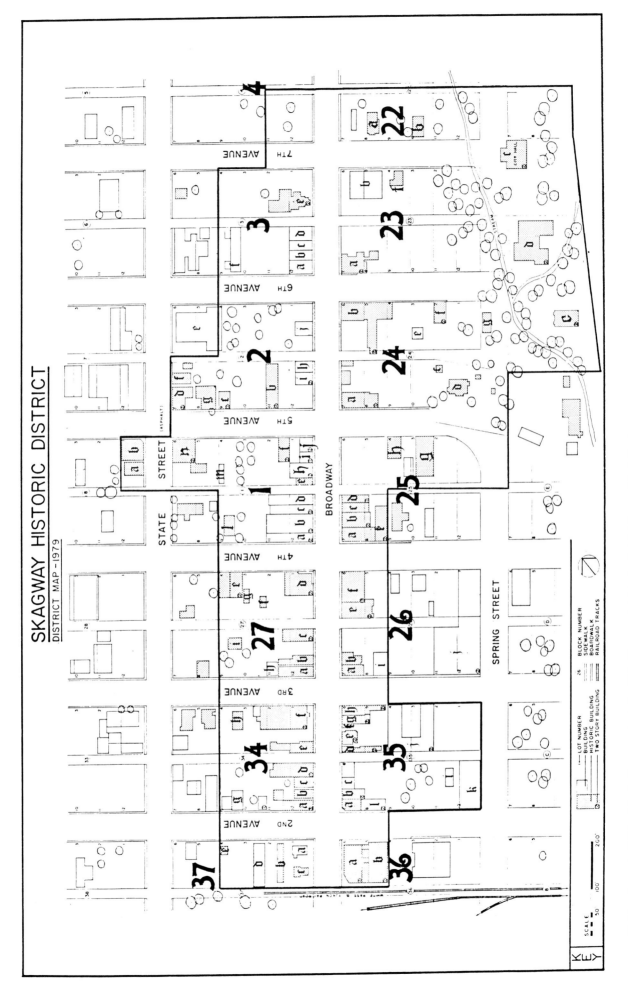

Gold rush era buildings (shaded) are protected within Skagway's historic district (heavy black line).

The railroad's first locomotive was brought north in 1898 after long service on the Utah and Northern Railroad. It was built in 1881, rebuilt in 1900, renumbered 352 and retired in 1940. It is being restored in 2003 by the White Pass Railroad.

Engine #195 was built in 1943 for use in Iran but was diverted to Skagway, converted to narrow-gauge and used until the end of the war. It has been moved north of city hall.

Restored engine #73 picking up passengers at the dock. The engine was built in 1947, retired in 1964 and restored in 1982 and 2003.

Broadway looking north from Third Avenue. Keller's Curio Shop was built in 1898 and served for years as a saloon and restaurant.

Broadway looking north from Second Avenue. Some of these buildings are on their original sites while others were moved here in the early 1900s.

Several buildings on Broadway's west side. The AB (Arctic Brotherhood) Hall was built in 1899 for the fraternal order. It has a façade of driftwood and sticks shaped into a mosaic of letters, gold pan and square patterns. President Warren G. Harding was the last initiated member of Camp Skagway No. 1 in 1923. It is owned by the city.

The Trail Inn and Pack Train Saloon building at Fourth and Broadway was originally an old army barracks and was moved to the site in 1908. The wood frame two-and-a-half story barracks was sawed in half and placed perpendicular to Broadway with a three-story false front added. A tower was placed in the corner. The building has been restored. Next door is the Lynch & Kennedy Dry Goods and Haberdashery, another army barracks building moved in 1908. It is owned by the NPS.

Skagway's city hall and Skagway Museum are located in the 1899 McCabe College building. It was constructed as Alaska's first institution of higher education and its first granite building. It was later used as a courthouse. An administration building addition was added in 2002 to the rear of the building.

The National Park Service's Visitors Center is now located in the 1898 White Pass and Yukon Route depot. Next door is the ornate 1900 railroad general office building, which now houses the administrative offices for the National Park Service. The buildings have been completely restored.

Jeff Smith's Parlor was constructed in 1897 as a bank building. It later became Soapy Smith's saloon and headquarters and after his death a restaurant. Martin Itjen moved it across Sixth Avenue in 1935 and George Rapuzzi moved it to its present location in 1964. It was operated for years by Itjen and Rapuzzi as a museum. One of Itjen's streetcars often sits beside the building.

A reminder of World War II is this barracks built for soldiers of the 770th Railway Operating Battalion. It is next to Jeff Smith's Parlor. It was a mess hall.

Skagway's largest dance hall and saloon was built as the Red Onion in 1898 on Sixth Avenue. In 1914 it was moved to its present location, with the back of the saloon facing Broadway and thus becoming the front. It is now a bar with a brothel museum upstairs.

The Mascot Saloon opened for business in 1898 and after Prohibition it became the Skagway Drug Store. Next door is the Pacific Clipper Line Office building, later to become part of the Mascot and drug store. Both buildings have been restored by the Park Service and now operate as Northwest Original (middle) and Gold Strike (right).

Kirmse Jewelry Store was built in 1899 and remodeled for the jewelry store in 1904. Herman Kirmse opened his first Pioneer Jewelry Store in 1897 on Sixth Avenue. The north portion was acquired in 1906. Kirmse's son Jack operated the business until 1977 when it was sold. It is still in operation today as Little Switzerland.

The Wells Fargo Bank building was constructed in 1916 at the corner of Sixth Avenue and Broadway. The U.S. Post Office occupies the north part of the building.

The Moore family homestead at Fifth and Spring streets, circa 1900, has been restored by the National Park Service and opened to the public.

Dedman's Photo Shop occupies this 1897 building, which was E.A. Hegg's photo studio from 1897 to 1901. The building has been altered several times.

The Eagles' Hall is made up of two 1898 hotels—The Mondamin and The Pacific, which were moved to the site between 1916-20. The facade was added in 1916. The Eagles acquired the building and remodeled it into a theater/hall. The "Days of 98" show is held here every summer. A new building has been built to the right.

Skagway's grandest hotel was the Golden North, which was built by the Klondike Trading Co. in 1898 as a business building. It was also used as an army barracks. In 1908 it was moved to its present site, a third floor added and opened as a hotel. It was restored after this photo was taken, and is now used for retail space and employee housing.

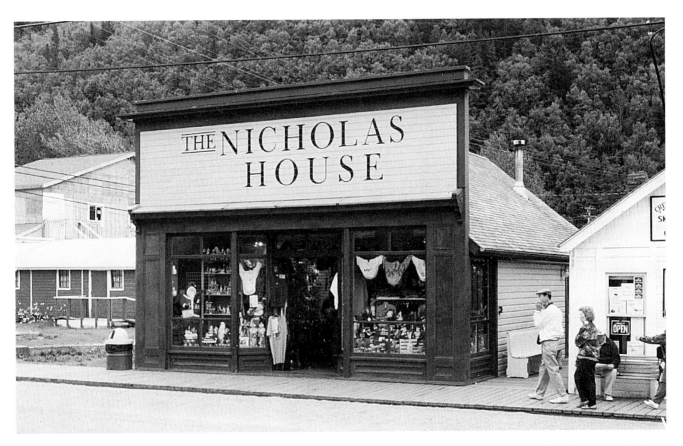

The 1897 Boss Bakery building sits on Broadway. It was originally built by Frank Brackett, son of the wagon-road builder George Brackett. It has been a trading post, bakery, restaurant and ice cream parlor. It was partially destroyed in World War II and has now been restored by the National Park Service.

Richter's Jewelry & Curio Shop has occupied this building since the late 1920s. The right-side portion was built in 1899 and used as a ticket office and later a restaurant. The middle portion was built by J. H. Richter in 1929 and the left side in 1972.

The Skagway Hardware building on the corner of Fourth and Broadway was built in 1900 as the Peterson & Co. mercantile. In 1909 the building was moved to its present location.

This building was built in 1899 as the Nome Saloon. An addition and false front were constructed and the building operated as a saloon and gambling hall for years. It is now a gift shop.

The Pantheon Saloon building is a hodgepodge of structure dating to 1897. It has been a flophouse, hardware store, saloon, restaurant and curio shop. Now owned by the National Park Service, it has been remodeled for retail businesses, the Alaska Fur Gallery and Princesses World Jewelers.

The Skagway Inn was built in 1918 by Max Gutfeld, operator of a bakery on Broadway, using materials from a gold rush era building. A vacant 1901 building was added in the rear in the 1920s.

Case-Mulvihill house on Seventh Avenue. Built in 1904 for W.H. Case of Case and Draper photographers. Long-time residence of W.J. Mulvihill, chief dispatcher of the White Pass & Yukon Route. The structure combines Victorian Gothic with Queen Anne details.

A reminder of the past from Skagway's fire department.

F. M. Woodruff, President

J. H. Kelly, Vice President

H. B. Le Fevre, Secretary

H. M. Lay, Treasurer

The
Skagway Chamber of Commerce

TRUSTEES

John Kalem

J. G. Price

W. H. Case

Frank Bishoprick

L. S. Keller

Skagway, Alaska,   1902

_____

_____

GENTLEMEN:—The people of Alaska have no voice in governmental affairs. They have no delegate in congress authorized to speak for them. Over 65,000 people have cast their lot in this new country, where they have established homes, and their main hope centers in the prosperity of the country.

Alaska is not a territory. It is but an outlying district or colony of the United States. Her people, playing no part in the councils of the nation, receive inadequate attention at the hands of a busy congress, the delegations of which are engrossed in the affairs of their enfranchised constituencies. The only hope, therefore, that the people of Alaska have of obtaining rights inalienable co-equal to those enjoyed by the free people of the United States, lies in the humanity and love of fairness of the citizens of the mother country. And your Honorable Body is, therefore, hereby respectfully solicited to pass for our benefit the enclosed, or memorial of similar intent, and send one copy to congress through a member of your congressional delegation, and to return two copies to this chamber that we may attach one to our general Alaskan petition, and retain one for the archives of this chamber, as a reminder in years to come of the gratitude we may owe to the represented citizens of the United States, who may have interceded in our behalf.

With this petition you will also find copies of extracts of reports, documents and press articles showing the importance of our country and the justice of our prayers.

Very respectfully,

The Skagway Chamber of Commerce,

By_____

Secretary.

-136-

ISSUED BY

WHITE PASS & YUKON ROUTE
Pacific & Arctic Railway and Navigation Co.
British Columbia Yukon Railway Co.
British Yukon Railway Co.
The British Yukon Navigation Co., Ltd.

GOOD FOR

ONE FIRST CLASS PASSAGE
To the point designated on Coupons attached when officially signed and stamped.

Subject to the Following Contract:

1st. In selling this Ticket and checking baggage hereon, this Company acts as Agent and is not responsible beyond its own line.

2d. No stop-over will be allowed unless permitted by local regulations of the lines over which this Ticket reads, and no Agent is authorized to make any representations as to what such regulations are; it may be exchanged by Conductors at any point for Tickets or Checks conforming to such regulations.

3d. It is Void for passage if any alterations or erasures are made hereon, or if more than one date is cancelled.

4th. If the Coupons are punched or marked SECOND CLASS, the passenger is entitled to Second-Class passage only, otherwise First-Class.

5th. If Limited as to time it will not be accepted for passage after date cancelled by "L" punch in margin hereof, and is subject to exchange, either in whole or part, at any point on the route, for a Continuous Passage Ticket, or Check.

6th. Baggage liability is limited to wearing apparel only not exceeding one hundred dollars in value.

7th. When this Ticket is signed below by the purchaser, or if time limited, it is not transferable, and if presented by any other person, that the original holder will be taken up and full fare collected.

8th. No one other than the person whose signature appears on the face of this Ticket as the purchaser thereof is entitled to passage, and any person presenting this Ticket will identify himself or herself as such person by writing his or her name, or by other means if necessary, when required by Conductors, Agents or Pursers.

9th. Should any occurrence prevent any steamer or conveyance from leaving at the appointed time or result in the loss or detention thereof, this Company shall not be held responsible for the maintenance of passengers nor for any loss resulting from such delay; and in case of substitution of steamers this Company reserves the right to berth the passengers by its Agents or Pursers.

10th. The Company does not provide board and lodging while awaiting conveyance.

11th. This Ticket is sold subject to the agreement of the purchaser to pay any tax payable for or on the purchaser under the laws of any country in which passage on this Ticket extends, and failure of the purchaser to do so, when requested by any Conductor or Agent of the Company, will render this Ticket void for passage in such country, and if, for any reason, the purchaser is prevented or delayed in entering such country by the laws thereof, or its officers, there shall be no liability on the Company, to the purchaser, for damages or otherwise.

12th. No Agent or Employe has power to modify this Contract in any particular.

* I hereby agree to all the conditions of the above contract.

Geo. M. Julien _____ PURCHASER

J. Warren _____ WITNESS

_____ AGENT

Form 102

A. L. Berry _____ GEN'L MGR.

238

1917
1916
1915
1914
1913
1912
1911
1910
1909

31	5
30	4
29	3
28	2
27	1
26	Dec Day
25	
24	Dec
23	Nov
22	Oct
21	S/o
20	
19	Sep
18	Aug
	July
16	June
15	May
14	
13	Apr
12	Mar
11	
10	Feb
9	
8	Jan
7	
6	

ISSUED BY

WHITE PASS & YUKON ROUTE
RAIL DIVISION

GOOD FOR

One FIRST Class Passage

* On conditions named in Contract.

FROM

WHITE HORSE
TO
SKAGUAY

Worthless if Detached

Form

238

FINAL DESTINATION SKAGUAY

O

ALASKA SOUTHERN WHARF CO.

Good for One Passage between

SKAGUAY and DYE

When stamped by Agent.

STEAMER LADY LAKE

White Pass & Yukon Route

Good for one continuous passage on date stamped on back

BENNETT
TO
SKAGUAY

Form 39

216

THE WHITE PASS & YUKON ROUTE
TRAFFIC DEPARTMENT

J. FRANCIS LEE,
TRAFFIC MANAGER
SEATTLE, WASH., AND
SKAGUAY, ALASKA

Skaguay July 21st 1902

Claim #697, Ames Merc. Co., Dawson,

Loss D. Fruit & Can Goods —

Dried Fruit amt. $5.13

Can'd Meats, etc. — " 14.20

Total. $19.33

Alaska Transfer Co
City.

Gentlemen:— Papers in the above numbered claim were transmitted you with my letter covering the subject matter of same under date of June 27th 1902 — Not having been returned by you to date, I need by glass if you would have the matter receive early attention & greatly oblige —

Yours Truly
J. Wilson
Car.

ON TOP OF THE WORLD — AT THE TOP OF THE WORLD

SOUVENIR OF YOUR FLIGHT
Over the CHILKOOT RANGE, from SKAGWAY, Alaska
In a Ford Tri-Motor Airplane
WHITE PASS AIRWAYS, Inc.

No. 1693   Date 6-22-1937   Pilot

Bibliography

Berton, Pierre, *Klondike, the Last Great Gold Rush, 1896-1899,* McClelland & Stewart Limited, Toronto, 1972.

Clifford, Howard, *The Skagway Story,* Alaska Northwest Publishing Co., Anchorage, 1975.

Clifford, Howard, *Doing the White Pass, the Story of the White Pass and Yukon Route and the Klondike Gold Rush,* Sourdough Enterprises, Seattle, 1983.

Itjen, Martin, *The Story of the Tour on the Skagway, Alaska Street Car,* published by the author, 1938.

Martin, Cy, *Gold Rush Narrow Gauge,* Trans-Anglo Books, Corona del Mar, California, 1973.

Moore, J. Bernard, *Skagway In Days Primeval,* Vintage Press, New York, 1968.

Spude, Robert L. S., *Skagway, District of Alaska, 1884-1912,* University of Alaska Occasional Paper #36, Fairbanks, 1983.

About the Author

Stan Cohen, a native of West Virginia, is a graduate geologist and spent two summers working in Alaska as a geologist for the U.S. Forest Service. Since 1976 he has spent part of every summer in Alaska and the Yukon researching and writing about the North Country. He established Pictorial Histories Publishing Company in 1976 and has since written 65 history books and published over 200. His North Country titles include: *The Streets Were Paved With Gold; The Forgotten War; The Trail of 42; The White Pass and Yukon Route; Yukon River Steamboats; Rails Across The Tundra; Alaska Wilderness Rails* and *Top Cover for America.* He lives in Missoula, Montana, with his wife, Anne.